Training the Best

Best wishes Linda
Charles D Flowers
5/25/05

Charles Herbert Flowers, Jr.
Tuskegee Airman Flight Instructor

Dorothy M. Poole

Training the Best

Charles Herbert Flowers, Jr.
Tuskegee Airman Flight Instructor

Dorothy M. Poole

Training the Best

Charles Herbert Flowers, Jr.
Tuskegee Airman Flight Instructor

Dorothy M. Poole

Robnor Publishing, LLC

Library of Congress Control Number   2008942509

ISBN 0-9776192-3-0

Photo Credits: Unless otherwise credited, all photos are from the collection of Charles Herbert Flowers, Jr. and the Flowers family. Every effort has been made to identify copyright holders.

Published by Robnor Publishing, LLC
Washington, D.C.

Contents

Dedication

This book is dedicated to Carolyn Elaine Flowers Green and to Charles Herbert Flowers, III by their parents, Charles and Wilhelmina. Without fail, Carolyn and Herbie have always been there to fill the void left by the deaths of their brother, Roderick Dean Flowers, and their sister, Beatrice Yvonne Flowers Hinton.

Acknowledgements

My thanks to Mr. Charles Herbert Flowers, Jr. for having the confidence in me to write his biography in spite of the fact that my only writing experience has been in conjunction with my career as a computer programmer/analyst. My thanks is also given to Mrs. Wilhelmina Flowers for her patience and graciousness through all the interviews and visits in their home. I would also like to acknowledge the advice, support and encouragement of my husband, Boyd Poole, throughout this challenging writing project.

Dorothy M. Poole

Introduction

Spirits are awaked within each student, parent or staff member who sights Mr. Charles Herbert Flowers entering the hallways, gymnasium, auditorium or stadium. His calm demeanor and ever-pleasant smile warms the hearts of those who respect and cherish his history, sacrifices and contributions. We stand to loudly and proudly salute the presence of this man of honor. When he speaks, a hush penetrates the air, as we hold on to his every word. Within the phrases that he utters, hope is instilled and respect is elevated, as we intently listen to his every word. At the conclusion of his delivery, crowds surround him and beg for autographs, hold his hand or just touch this magnificent hero. His smile broadens, as he stands still to honor their requests or recognizes their presence.

As principal of the school named for this great and proud man, I often refer to his history to inspire students to work with diligence for success to show their appreciation and respect for his exceptional accomplishments. I was deeply honored when he requested me to remain as principal for as long as he lived. Although I did not agree, my unspoken promise motivates me to strive to continue to build a "Mecca of Excellence" for his name sake. His confidence in me serves as the catalyst for my commitment to continue to honor the man who inspires our hopes and fulfills our dreams.

Mrs. Helena Nobles-Jones, Principal
Charles Flowers High School

Chapter 1

The Early Years

Charles Herbert Flowers, Jr. was born on August 8, 1918, in a family house on a farm in Anson County, North Carolina. Many of his close friends have always called him "Herb." He was the first born and only child of Charles Herbert Flowers, Sr. and Ola Huntley Flowers. Since the economy was based on farming at this time, having just one child was unusual. Having large families insured that there would be enough farm hands to grow and harvest crops for income and food.

This was the case for Herb's grandparents on both sides because the William Flowers family had eleven children and the John Huntley family had ten. Herb's paternal and maternal grandparents were all born during slavery which did not end until 1865 when the 13th Amendment to the Constitution was ratified even though the Emancipation Proclamation was signed in 1863.

Herb's parents, however, were born more than 25 years after slavery ended. His father, Charles Herbert Flowers, Sr. was born in Anson County, North Carolina, in 1892 to William Flowers and Mary Ann Marshall. His mother, Ola Huntley Flowers, was born in Anson County, North Carolina, in 1894 to John Huntley and Lula Brewer Huntley.

In spite of their humble beginnings, Herb's grandparents on both sides (the Flowers' and the Huntley's) did well economically. Undoubtedly, some of their good fortunes had to do with the fact that they all had good educations. The Huntley's were both high school graduates. The Flowers had both completed the seventh grade. This was a solid level of educational attainment and literacy for that era.

Herb's maternal grandparents, the Huntley's, had a large farm and owned two cars (one of them was a Cadillac). They had one of the successful farms in that area and grew corn, sugar cane and cotton.

His paternal grandparents, William Flowers and Mary Ann Marshall Flowers, owned a big house and 150 acres and grew corn, sugar cane and cotton, also. Cotton was the cash crop of that era. (The soil in Anson County was sandy and more suitable for growing cotton than tobacco.) Other crops grown on the farm were used to feed the family.

There were several other Black farmers who

owned large farms in Anson County (George Baucham, Abraham Clemmons, Henry Marsh, to name a few), but not all Black families in Anson County were so fortunate. Many of these families were making a living by share cropping on land owned by white land owners who themselves had been former slave owners. The only difference between the lot of the share croppers and that of slaves was that sharecroppers were supposedly being compensated for their labor. However, by the time that the land owners deducted the rent for the broken down shacks that they lived in and the charges for their basic food rations, there were very few nickels and dimes left to be paid to the sharecroppers for their labor.

Charles H. Flowers, Sr. and Ola Huntley both attended Lincoln Academy, a normal school, in Kings Mountain, N. C. A Normal school was an advanced place of learning for students of that time. It was similar to a high school, but the training received there was more advanced than that of a high school of today. They met there in 1915. They had lived about 20 miles apart in Anson County and had not known each other prior to attending Lincoln Academy.

Charles, Sr. drove his horse and buggy when calling on Ola. After about 2 years of courting and after each received certification for teaching, they married in 1917 (Ages 25 and 23). William Flowers thought a lot of his daughter-in-law, Ola. He welcomed her and Charles to live in one of the two extra houses located on his farm. (Herb's aunt, Charles Sr.'s younger sister, lived in the other house). Charles Herbert Flowers, Jr. (Herb) was born in that house. He was a healthy 10 pound baby. It is quite possible that a difficult labor precipitated by a large baby could have been one of the reasons that his mother chose not to have any more children.

During their early years of marriage, both of Herb's parents taught in Anson County Public Schools. His father taught at the White Pond Elementary School in the Streeters Grove area of the county and his mother taught at the Gatewood Station Elementary School in the Morven area of Anson. During the time that Herb was a toddler, she did not have a baby sitter, so she took him to school with her. He attended school with his mother from the tender age of three. This early childhood education experience helped him skip at least two elementary school grades.

Charles Sr.'s mother, Mary Ann, passed away in 1922. By that time, he was the only child still living on the family farm. In 1923, Charles decided to move on as his brothers and sisters had done, so he, Ola and Herb moved to Hamlet, North Carolina. Charles, Sr. was then working as an insurance agent for North Carolina Mutual Insurance Company, a highly successful African American Insurance company located in Durham, N. C. In her book, *The Inventive Spirit of African Americans*, Patricia Carter Sluby states, " A few visionary Africans in 1899 organized the North Carolina Mutual and Provident Association, subsequently changing its name to the North Carolina Mutual Life Insurance Company, which survived the great crash and the depression due to the brilliant leadership of its president, C.C. Spaulding....it became the largest African American business in the United States..[and] flourishes today." Ola got a teaching job at an elementary school in Hamlet and Charles and Ola became home owners for the first time when they built a new house.

By this time, Herb was old enough to go to school and he attended an elementary school which had at least three rooms. His grades were always good and he skipped at least one grade while attending school in Hamlet. His only problem at school was with the bullies. He often got into fights with them because he was just not going to be pushed around.

When he was at home, he played with his friends, Lowell and Talbot Darby, who lived across the street. He wasn't allowed to wander too far from his own yard, so it was good that he got along so well with the brothers who lived across the street. Their friendship made up for not having any siblings or of having any of his cousins nearby.

Training the Best

Misfortune struck Charles and Ola in 1926 when their house in Hamlet burned down. After that happened, the family moved to Fayetteville, North Carolina. Charles, Sr. was still working for North Carolina Mutual and Ola got a teaching job in Fayetteville. They lived in Fayetteville for about three years.

The elementary school there was larger than any that Herb had ever attended. And because of his friendliness, he had lots of friends there and he continued to make good grades. Math was his favorite subject and his dream was to become a doctor so that he could cure sick people.

In Fayetteville, Herb was older and allowed to venture farther away from his home. His close friends were Harry and Kermit Fleming, Earl McMillan and Archie Banks. They played ball and shot marbles together. They also spent a lot of time on "tom walkers," better known as stilts. Herb was exceptionally good at that. One day when Herb was on stilts about six feet off the ground walking along Gillespie Street, he met a white woman who was so impressed with his stilt walking skills that she stopped him and handed him fifty cents! Fifty cents was a lot of money for a child to have in those days and that made him a very happy young man.

While living in Fayetteville and at the tender age of nine, Herb learned how to drive the family car, which at that time was a Nash. He used to go with his father to collect insurance premiums from his father's insurance customers. Herb would drive the car between house stops. Believe it or not, there were no legal restrictions on driving at that time. If you owned a car and could reach both the steering wheel and the pedals at the same time, you could drive. Driver's license requirements were not put into effect in North Carolina until some time in the mid 1930's.

In 1929, Herb's paternal grandfather, William Flowers, died. Some time prior to his death, William sold all but 20 acres of his farm land to a white farmer whose land was adjacent to his. These 20 acres were to be divided between his children. Charles, Sr. and Ola decided to move back to Anson County to become farmers. Herb's father, Charles Sr., who was William's youngest, bought the family farm shares of his siblings so that he could have sole ownership of the farm. Then he became a full time farmer raising 15 acres of cotton for the cash support of his family and 5 acres of food crops. He grew corn, wheat, peas, onions, sweet potatoes, white potatoes, and string beans for food for the family and oats for feeding the mule and the pigs. Charles, Ola and Herb were the only workers on the farm. Herb's father did most of the planting. Herb helped with cultivating the crops and fed and cared for the mule and pigs. His mother took care of the chickens and her cow. They all pitched in to harvest the crops.

The family only had to buy staples such as sugar and salt. Since Herb's mother did not sew, they also had to buy clothing.

In addition to helping on the farm, Herb's mother continued her teaching career. She taught at Gatewood Station Elementary School in Anson County. The school had three rooms, two teachers and a principal who also served as the head master teacher. The school had grades one thru seven. The majority of children during that time completed only the seventh grade before dropping out of school.

The school year was for seven months, from October to April. This shortened school year allowed the children of farmers to help their families with farming chores and insured that families would be able to survive. Even with the shortened school year, some children were kept out of school by their parents so that they could help with the farming chores. Herb's parents knew the value of having a good education, so he was required to go to school everyday. They never kept him out of school to help out on the farm. Herb did not do any chores before school. Primarily, he did his chores after school. For Herb, growing up on a farm was tough, especially having to pick so much cotton because he didn't have any siblings to help with this chore.

The Flowers' family attended Gatewood Station AME Zion Church. Ola sang in the church choir and was active in the Women's church group.

Charles, Sr. was the superintendent of Sunday school. They lived close to the church and were able to walk there, so there was no need to drive the family car which at that time was a Model A Ford.

High School and College

Herb was in the eighth grade when his family returned to Anson County. He entered Anson County Training School in Wadesboro North Carolina. It was the high school for blacks (Schools of that era were segregated). This school was larger than one that he had attended in Fayetteville. Even though this was a bigger and better school than any that he had attended, it wasn't as good as the white high school. There were inequities that existed between the white school system and the black school system during this era. Many state and local governments, especially in the South, had long standing policies of not allocating the same per capita funding for black students and schools as they did for whites, usually black school received much less funding. There were differences in the duration of the school year. Another difference was that white children rode buses to their schools and black children had to walk to theirs. This walk was many miles for most black children, but Herb was fortunate in that he was either driven or sometimes drove himself to school.

Being back in Anson County was good for Herb. He had his cousins, Vernel, Hubert and Charles to look out for him at school and in the neighborhood. Vernel was the same age as Herb and was his closest pal. Also, he had cousins Clarence and Marie Flowers, and Joleitha Bennett at Anson County Training School to make up a close circle of classmates who were family as well as friends.

His cousin, Joleitha, never let him forget about the incident with his mother's cow. It seems that one day the cow was in the family pea patch eating peas. Herb's father asked him to run the cow out of the pea patch and Herb did as he was told. The cow went back into the patch again and Herb's father said, "Son, I want you to go out there and kill that cow!" Herb went outside and found an oak grub (a large root with a handle). He took aim and threw it at the cow striking the cow between the horns and the cow keeled over. The county animal doctor, Ray Horn, was called and he came over and pronounced the cow dead. The cow was cut into beef steaks and Herb had his first steak ever. News traveled fast in that little community and everyone around heard about the cow incident by the next day, which was Sunday. So, Herb gained an unwelcome amount of attention from his friends and neighbors for his role in the death of his mother's cow. He never intended to kill that cow. Of course, his mother was very upset that her cow was dead but it was not the end of the world even though she did love that cow. In time, she bought another cow to replace the one she lost.

The principal of Anson County Training School was the Reverend J. R. Faison. He was a Baptist minister and of course had a strict code of conduct like most southern Baptist ministers. So students at Anson County Training School had to be on their best behavior at all times. Since Herb's father was a strict disciplinarian and Herb was used to towing the line, he got along very well with the principal. Principal Faison even made Herb his chauffeur. The principal's car was a Hudson Essex and Herb certainly didn't mind driving it. Also, Principal Faison needed a typist, so he made Herb his typist even though he was not a trained typist. Herb had taught himself to type by the hunt and peck method. He was a resourceful young man willing to take on any challenge.

Herb made good grades throughout high school. His favorite subject was math just as it had been in elementary school and he added biology as another favorite. His dream of becoming a doctor did not change during his high school years. Flying and aviation were not part of his career goals at that point in his life.

At Herb's senior prom, dancing was not allowed by Principal Faison. Southern Baptists' looked upon dancing as a sin so the students had to march instead. Herb didn't mind because he couldn't dance, anyway, and his prom date would not have to be disappointed about his lack of dancing skills.

Herb completed the 12th grade at the age of 15; he had gotten ahead of his peers in his classes because he skipped grades. He graduated from Anson County Training School in June 1934 and was the class salutatorian. Herb won a full two-year scholarship to A&T College of North Carolina in Greensboro.[1]

Herb entered A&T in the fall of 1934 at the age of sixteen as a premed major. He was still wearing knee pants. At that time, the dress for boys younger than seventeen was knickers or knee pants and socks that came to the knees. The girls on campus referred to Herb as "little brother." He probably reminded them of their younger brothers at home.

Although Herb had no prior music training, he took an interest in the A&T marching band. In his freshman year, he became acquainted with the band

---

[1] A & T College of North Carolina became North Carolina A & T State University in 1967.

master who gave Herb music lessons in playing the E Flat Bass Tuba. Herb was a good music student who practiced diligently.

During the summer break after his freshman year, Herb got a job in Durham, North Carolina waiting tables to make money to help finance his education.

In the fall, Herb returned to A & T as a sophomore. By this time, Herb was playing the E Flat Bass Tuba well enough to make 1st band. As in all his prior years in school, Herb made good grades in all of his subjects. In spite of his success in school, Herb felt that something was missing. He felt that his youth and lack of experience put him at a disadvantage.

Herb left A&T after completing his sophomore year. His scholarship had run out and he didn't want to burden his parents with the expense of his remaining two years of college.

That summer after leaving A&T, Herb got a job in Durham washing dishes at K&W Restaurant. While there, he heard about Army Air Corps recruiters coming to visit Duke University's campus to recruit high school graduates for the Army Air Corps. Herb decided to go to one of the recruiting sessions. He thought that joining the Air Corps would be a great opportunity to gain experience and earn money to pay for his last two years of college. The recruiters laughed at him and said, "Boy, you know there are no colored boys flying in the Air Corps." Needless to say, Herb was very disappointed but knew not to let his true feelings show.

After working in Durham for a little over a year, Herb decided to move on. He wanted to gain more life experience before returning to school. So, he contacted some cousins in Baltimore, Maryland. They agreed to let him come there and stay with them while he looked for a place of his own. He arrived in Baltimore and after one week, he found a room to rent for three to four dollars a week. He got a job driving a delivery truck for a clothing manufacturer, Saul Rosenbloom. (Saul's son, Carol Rosenbloom later became the owner of the then Baltimore Colts football team).

In the spring of 1941, Herb was told by some home buddies about an article in the Norfolk Journal and Guide (An African American Newspaper) which detailed the new program established by President Roosevelt for the training of Negro pilots for the Army Air Corps. Herb immediately went out to buy a copy of the newspaper because this program was a very big deal.

During this era, questions remained about the suitability of blacks as aircraft pilots in general and fighter pilots particularly, in the mindset of America. Fundamental questions about their courage, intellect, and resourcefulness remained and were supposedly documented in studies commissioned by the War

Department and War College. Twice, once in 1925 and again in 1937, the War College commissioned studies that concluded that "blacks were cowards, and poor technicians and fighters..." But because of war preparation for World War II, the politics of the day, and common sense, the War Department stated that blacks would be called into service in proportion to their percentage of the population, but would be segregated, and would not be eligible for the Army Air Corps.

The Presidential election of 1940 provided an opportunity for the issue of segregation and blacks in the armed services to receive more serious thought and debate than it had previously received. Wendell L. Willkie, the Republican candidate, promised to integrate the Armed Forces if elected causing President Roosevelt to take action on the issue during late 1940. Previously, in 1938, Roosevelt had approved $100,000 of National Youth Administration funds for Civilian Pilot Training Programs (CPTP) at thirteen colleges and universities in the United States. In 1939 after the Nazis invaded Poland, $7 million of additional funds were appropriated.

In December 1940, the War Department submitted a plan for an "experiment" involving black pilots. But the Army Air Corps still refused applications from blacks until Yancey Williams, a Howard University student, filed a suit through the NAACP in 1941. Then in March 1941, the Selective

Service Headquarters said in part, "The Negro pilots will be trained at Tuskegee, Alabama, in connection with Tuskegee Institute…" Shortly thereafter a training center was established there.

By February 1941, Tuskegee Institute had received certification to provide advanced flying courses and would soon receive $1.7 million for an air field. When speaking with the Pittsburgh Courier, once the nation's most widely distributed black newspaper, during the spring of 1941 about the Tuskegee Pilot project and what considerations blacks should use for choosing candidates for the program, Major General Waller R. Weaver, the commander of the Army's Southeastern Air Corps Training Command, pleaded: "For God's sake, send us your best men…For their sake and for our sake, give us your best."

These developments worked in favor of Charles Flowers, Jr.; the opportunity which he had previously sought and had been denied was now open to him. This program for black pilots would be his ticket to funding a return to college to complete his college education and it would also satisfy his draft requirements. Up to this time, blacks were a part of a segregated military and were consigned to mediocre and menial task units. This new opportunity with the Army Air Corps had been brought about by years of lobbying Congress and the President by black aviators and their white supporters and also by the need for more pilots to conduct the air war in World War II.[2]

The minimum requirement for the Negro recruits was two years college which Herb had. He only had to pass a rigorous physical examination to become a recruit. In April of 1941 on Easter Monday morning, he took a seven and a half hour rigorous physical test at the local armory. He was one of two Negro applicants to pass the physical. This test had to be a piece of cake for a young man raised on a farm and made physically fit by all that hard labor. Herb's parents were as excited as he was about his becoming a recruit for the Army Air Corps.

---

[2] Negro Airmen International, Inc. (NAI): 4/9/2007
<http://www.blackwings.com/history.html>

Training the Best

Aviation Cadet Captain Flowers

Herb's orders to report to Tuskegee came in August of 1941. At that time, he had to take another physical examination which he passed as easily as he did the first one. In September, 1941, he reported to Tuskegee. He was placed in the third class of recruits. There were ten cadets in this class and all except Herb had college degrees. The cadet classes at Tuskegee were started at ten-week intervals and each class lasted 30-35 weeks.

The first class was designated 42-C and contained 12 students. Lt. Benjamin O. Davis, a West Point graduate, was in that first class. He was being groomed by the Army to become the leader of the 99th Pursuit squadron – the first of the Tuskegee Airmen squadrons. The second class was 42-D and contained 10 students. Herb's class of 10 was designated 42-E. In this class designation structure, the numbers represented the year, and alphabets the month, so Herb successfully completed all phases of pilot training and graduated in May of 1942.

At the beginning of the Tuskegee aviation program, the cadets lived in the temporary quarters and there was no defined runway on Moton Airfield, which was the field used for primary training. The program was in its infancy and the facilities at Tuskegee were rudimentary. Congress appropriated money for improvements to the aviation facilities. Permanent barracks for the cadets were completed by March 1942 at the Tuskegee Army Air Field (TAAF) and Moton Field was improved.

There were four phases of training for the aviation cadets. The first phase was Pre-Flight Training which consisted of 5 weeks of Ground School including classes on airplanes and engines, aerodynamics, navigation and meteorology, Morris code, and a physical training course which consisted mainly of calisthenics and close-order drills or drills in maneuvers, marching, and handling arms.

The second phase was Primary Flight Training which was 10 weeks of fundamental flight training on a PT-17 Kaydet plane which was a biplane and one of the earliest trainers used. During this training phase, half a day was used for flying and half was spent in classes, with an hour of physical training in the morning. Cadets would perform take-offs and landings. They learned the fundamentals of flying, how to operate the controls, how to fly the planes solo, and they went through a proscribed group of maneuvers for the first twenty hours. Herb was the first in his class to fly solo. Those who completed this phase of training graduated to Basic Flight Training. Those who didn't were said to have "washed out" and had to leave the program.

The third phase, Basic Flight Training was 10 weeks of flying solo and learning more of the same things as in primary flight training except the cadets flew a heavier plane, the BT-13. At this stage of the program cadets trained on planes with more speed, and adjustable propeller pitch for the first time. Cadets were also operating planes with two-way radios for the first time and planes that were much heavier, probably 2,000 pounds heavier with a much larger engine than those used in Primary Training. Another consideration in basic training was that cadets had to master all of the instruments available to them at this point.

The fourth and final phase was Advanced Flight Training. This phase consisted of 12 weeks of solo flying in the (Advance Trainer) AT-6. Herb was the top cadet in his class and was promoted to Aviation Cadet Captain. He was the second cadet to gain this distinction. The cadets performed Aerial maneuvers, the planes were much faster, a lot more maneuverable and flying was more enjoyable. At this stage, the instructors were trying to get them oriented to flying a fighter plane. Cadets also made a lot of cross-country trips during advanced flying - some at night - and longer cross-countries during the day. Cadets received aerial gunnery training at Elgin Air Force Base in Val Pariso, Florida during the final two weeks of the training period. Herb and his buddy, Bernard Knighten, set a record for the number of targets hit. Herb was first in the ground targets hit and second to Bernard in the number of plane-towed or aerial targets hit. For their excellence in aviation skills, they won a case of beer which they shared with their classmates.

Only five cadets from Herb's class of 10 completed all four phases of pilot training. In May 1942, Charles Herbert Flowers, Jr., Bernard Knighten, Sherman White, George Knox, and Lee Raeford graduated from the Tuskegee Army Air Corps flight school. Four of the other cadets washed out in Primary Flight Training and one washed out in Basic Flight Training. (The first class of cadets had five graduates including Lt. Benjamin O. Davis and the second class of cadets had three graduates.) So the total number of Tuskegee Aviation graduates by May 1942 came to thirteen.[3] Therefore, Herb was one of the first thirteen original Tuskegee Airmen.

---

[3] Some 994 cadets completed all phases of the Army Air Corps Pilot training program conducted at Tuskegee Institute between 1942 and 1946.

Aviation Cadet Captain Flowers

There was a shortage of flight instructors in the Tuskegee Flight Program at this time. The Army was looking for qualified flight instructors to fill that need. Colonel Frederick V. H. Kimble, the commanding officer of the Army Air Corps Advanced Flying School at Tuskegee at that time, was so impressed with Herb's flying abilities, that he chose him to become a flight instructor instead of being assigned to a flight duty station.[4]

Herb was disappointed on one hand that he would not get to go serve with pilot buddies with whom he had trained, but on the other hand he was happy to be a part of a great team of highly skilled pilots who would be teaching those who would eventually go to war or to other military duty stations. (Bernard Knighten was sent to Europe and survived the war. Sherman White was sent to Europe and was killed in action. George Knox and Lee Raeford were stationed at Tuskegee.)

---

[4] Col Frederick V. H. Kimble, a West Point Graduate, was the commanding officer of the Army Air Corps Advanced Flying School at Tuskegee from January 1942 – December 1942. In December 1942, he was replaced by Lieutenant Colonel Noel F. Parrish.

Civilian Pilot Instructors

The assignment as a flight instructor changed Herb's status with the military. He became a civilian flight instructor. At the time Herb was assigned to the instructor group, there were only four primary flight instructors at Tuskegee Army Air Field and they were all civilian trained. The civilian flight instructors were employed by Tuskegee Institute. The Army Air Corps wanted military-trained flight instructors to be a part of the civilian flight instructors' group and Herb became the "First Military Trained African American Primary Flight Instructor." He was given an Honorable Discharge from the Army Air Corps. Two other Army Air Corps aviation graduates from later classes were chosen to become civilian flight instructors, also: John H. Young, III of the fourth cadet class and

Russell Harris of the fifth cadet class.

Part of the plan for the Tuskegee Aviation Program was that Blacks would be involved in all phases of aviation. The Civilian Pilot Training Program (CPTP), which had generally provided the training to the civilian instructors prior to Herb's assignment as an instructor, was taught at six Black educational institutions: Tuskegee Institute, Howard University, Hampton Institute, West Virginia State, Lincoln University (Pennsylvania) and A&T College at Greensboro. Mechanics, Air Traffic Controllers, Parachute Riggers and Avionic Technicians were trained at Chanute Air Base in Rantoul, Illinois.

Of the four Civilian Primary Flight Instructors at Tuskegee, two did not go thru the CPTP. One of them was Chief Charles Alford Anderson who taught himself to fly. Against all odds, Anderson became a pilot at a time when many roadblocks were set up to keep blacks from learning how to fly. In the early 1940s it was an accepted American stereotype that Blacks were not smart enough to learn to fly an airplane. Chief Anderson earned a pilots license in 1929 and was the first African-American to earn a pilots license. Chief Anderson later became known as the Father of Modern Black Aviation. In 1934, he and Dr. Albert E. Forsythe made several pan-American flights. Anderson was the pilot who took Eleanor Roosevelt on a flight when she visited Tuskegee. He became the chief pilot instructor of the primary flight instructors. Chief Anderson welcomed Herb into the group with open arms.

The other three civilian flight instructors were: Charles R. Fox (Tuskegee Grad of CPTP); Milton P. Crenshaw (Tuskegee Grad of CPTP) and Forrest Shelton. Forrest Shelton was a white pilot who trained outside of the CPTP. There was a great need for more flight instructors so others were added to this group as soon as they became available.

A Tuskegee Aviation Cadet's first flight experience at Tuskegee occurred with one of the civilian flight instructors.[5] White military instructors taught the Basic and Advanced Flight classes when Herb began teaching Primary Flight classes. Before actually starting as a flight instructor, Herb performed six more weeks of flight practice on his own. At the end of this extended training, he took a test for his commercial pilot's license, his flight instructor's rating and his instrument rating. He took these tests at Tuskegee with the Civil Aeronautics Authority Flight Inspector. Needless to say, he passed all these tests. In July 1942, Herb began working as a flight instructor.

Each primary flight instructor had a maximum of five cadets to train at one time. There was some risk in training these cadets to fly. Occasionally, a cadet would freeze and lock the controls and the

---

[5] Over 1,000 Army Air Corps cadets received their primary flight instruction from the Civilian Flight Instructors under the direction of Chief Anderson.

instructor would have trouble regaining control of the plane. However, there were never any crashes during flight training at Tuskegee. The only time a deadly crash occurred was during a flight formation exercise. In 1944, a flight instructor who had not been trained in formation flying and a cadet trainee attempted a formation with another inexperienced cadet flying solo and they crashed in mid-air. The flight instructor and the cadet flying with him were killed. The cadet flying solo survived. Perhaps this tragic accident could have been avoided if one of the military trained flight instructors had been flying in this exercise instead. All cadet pilots who completed all phases of the Army Air Corps flight training could execute formation flying. (The military basic and advanced flight classes required this.)

Because of the dire need for flight instructors, the CPT Program in the six black colleges began increasing the output in the number of pilots, by 1943 about 8 to 10 flight instructors, by 1944 there were about 12, and by 1945, there were about 20 primary flight instructors. Some of these flight instructors were trained by Cornelius Coffey at his air field located in Chicago. He had a contract to provide training for the CPT Program and trained eight or nine flight instructors for Tuskegee.

Chapter 5

Love, Marriage and Life at Tuskegee

Herb's future wife, Wilhelmina, was born May 20, 1923 in South Carolina to Reverend Julius Little and Alice Fountain Little. Her family moved to Wadesboro, North Carolina when Wilhelmina was about 4 years old. She had two brothers and four sisters. She was one of the middle children. Her father was the pastor of Brown Creek Baptist Church in Wadesboro. He also was a farmer, so she lived and worked on a farm as most children did at that time.

She attended Anson County Training School for a year or so before her family moved to Monroe, North Carolina where she would complete high school. Her family moved to Monroe when her father became the pastor of Friendship Baptist Church. They lived in the church parsonage. Her mother died in 1939 and not long after the family moved to Monroe. Some time later, her father, Reverend Little, married Herb's aunt, his mother's sister, Jeretha Huntley. Jeretha moved into the parsonage in Monroe with her new family. This family union would prove fateful for it brought Herb in contact with his future bride, Wilhelmina Little.

One Sunday evening in the latter part of 1941, Herb drove his mother, Ola, to visit her sister, Jeretha, in Monroe. Wilhelmina was very impressed with Herb and got permission from her parents to go for a ride with Herb. The car was his father's Ford. At that time, Herb had orders to report to Tuskegee so they would not see each other again for some time.

In the mean time, while Herb trained and then taught in Tuskegee, Wilhelmina attended DeShazors Beauty School in Durham and did her hair apprenticeship in Charlotte, North Carolina. Herb had been teaching at Tuskegee for a year before he would see Wilhelmina again.

Herb was on leave and he took a train to Charlotte, and from Charlotte he was to take a bus to Wadesboro. It just so happened that Wilhelmina was at that same bus station in Charlotte. At this time, Wilhelmina's sister was Miss Homecoming at Fayetteville State College in Fayetteville, North Carolina and Wilhelmina was going to Fayetteville to attend the homecoming activities. Herb was in his Civilian Pilot's Uniform: Riding Habit, Boots,

Military Jacket and Cap with an insignia. Wilhelmina took notice of the young man in that eye catching uniform. Immediately, she recognized the dashing man in uniform and tapped him on the shoulder. Herb was happy to see her. Just before they got on their respective buses, Herb said to Wilhelmina, "Come on back. Don't stay the weekend." Wilhelmina stayed in Fayetteville until early Sunday and returned to Wadesboro that day as Herb had requested.

Herb's mother was delighted to have her visit since she had been trying very hard to get the two of them together. She had encouraged their relationship. His mother thought that Herb had some interest in another girl in Wadesboro that she didn't approve of, but nothing was going on there on Herb's part. Herb drove Wilhelmina back to Charlotte in his daddy's car that evening so that she could go to work the next day. (Fate surely must have arranged this chance meeting because Herb was supposed to have taken an earlier train from Tuskegee but he missed it because he had left his wallet at his quarters. He took the train on the following day and that set the stage for him to run into Wilhelmina at the bus station in Charlotte).

Herb and Wilhelmina courted by mail; they only saw each other about twice during their year long courtship. Herb proposed marriage by letter and Wilhelmina answered his proposal by letter.

Without hesitation, she wrote back accepting his proposal. Their families planned their wedding and they were married by Reverend Sherman S. Thomas in August, 1943, in the parsonage in Monroe. Herb spent a week in Wadesboro before returning to Tuskegee.

By this time Herb had his own car. He drove back to Tuskegee to make preparations for his new bride's arrival. A short time later, Wilhelmina's step mother, Jeretha, and Wilhelmina's sister, Mildred, took her to Charlotte to catch an Eastern Airlines plane to Tuskegee. This was her first flight. Her sister was very nervous and raised her arms and said, "Oh, Lord Jesus. Oh, Lord Jesus, I'm not going to ever see my sister again." Wilhelmina was not afraid because she was too much in love and in a hurry to get to Tuskegee.

Their first residence was in Dorothy Hall, a two-story brick structure on the campus of Tuskegee Institute that housed married Tuskegee Airmen couples. After living on campus they rented a room from a couple for about a month. Then they rented an apartment in Greenwood Village. Wilhelmina and Herb were expecting their first child in June. When time came for Wilhelmina to deliver, Herb and two other civilian pilot friends, Wendell Lipscomb and Russell Harris, were in the hospital waiting for the baby to be born. Wilhelmina was screaming as loud as she could. The windows were open and she could be heard all over campus. The two friends were walking the hall and Herb was sitting in a chair. The nurse came out and asked who the father was. The two friends both said: "He's that fool sitting over there." Herb was the calm, reserved type and saw no need to pace and fret, so he just sat and waited patiently. Their first child, Carolyn Elaine Flowers, was born June 11, 1944, in John A. Andrews Memorial Hospital on the campus of Tuskegee Institute.

Wendell Lipscomb was from California. He was the one who started calling Herb "Tiger." It was a nickname that stuck. One could only assume that it was descriptive of the fearless pilot that Herb had become.

Russell Harris was from North Wilkesboro, North Carolina and when Russell saw a picture of Wilhelmina's sister, Mildred, on her stereo, he asked who she was. He said, "Pee Wee, who's this?" (They had given Wilhelmina the nickname of Pee Wee). She said, "That's my sister." He said, "Is she married?" "Nah," she said. He said, "I'm going to go get her" and he did just that. He went to North Carolina and wooed and won Mildred and they got married. Mildred and Russell moved to Tuskegee. The two couples bought a house together in Carver Court in 1944. (This was after Carolyn was born). The sisters were happy to be together again.

Wilhelmina really enjoyed her life at Tuskegee.

Training the Best

There were about fifty new homes in their community, and everyone knew everyone else. According to another pilot who lived there, "Those of us who were married and living in that community began living very charmed lives. We'd go in to work together, have parties on the weekend, and would go to the officers club together in between. We had a wonderful time. I worked as a flight instructor and we lived there until the military closed." Sometimes while the husbands were at work, the wives played bridge. These were exciting times for Wilhelmina and Mildred, two small town girls. The families were all so very close. Herb and Wilhelmina were close friends with Chief Anderson and his wife.

Herb bought Wilhelmina's first pair of high heeled shoes. She was nineteen at the time. He was trying to make her look more mature and sophisticated. They had to shop in Montgomery and Atlanta because there were no good places to shop in Tuskegee. So, how did they get to Montgomery and Atlanta? They flew, of course.

Herb and Wilhelmina took Sunday flights in a piper cub. They flew over Tuskegee with one holding the baby and the other at the controls. Herb taught and let Wilhelmina take the controls and fly the plane while they were in the air. She did not take off or land the plane, however.

Since there were no reputable stores or shops in Tuskegee, the pilots and their wives had little reason to come in contact with the white people of Tuskegee. Therefore, Herb and Wilhelmina encountered no racial incidents of significance there.

However, the Freeman Field Base located in Indiana had a severe problem with racial discrimination from both the townspeople – some of whom would not sell them groceries or provide laundry services - and the military brass that segregated them and treated them poorly. The Blacks officers stationed there were not allowed in the Officers Club. These were men who had served in combat during the war. They were upset that they faced discrimination in the military after serving their country in the war.

The war ended August 14, 1945. The Tuskegee Aviation program had been an astounding success.

The 99th Fighter Squadron was sent to North Africa in April 1943 for combat duty. They were joined by the 100th, 301st, and 302nd Black fighter squadrons. Together these squadrons formed the 332nd fighter group. The transition from training to actual combat wasn't always smooth given the racial tensions of the time. However, the Airmen overcame the obstacles posed by segregation. Under the able command of Col. Benjamin O. Davis, Jr., the well-trained and highly motivated 332nd flew successful missions over Sicily, the Mediterranean, and North Africa.

Bomber crews named the Tuskegee Airmen "Red Tail Angels" after the red tail markings on their aircraft. Also known as 'Black' or "Lonely Eagles," the German Luftwaffe called them 'Black Bird Men.' Many Tuskegee Airmen flew in the Mediterranean theater of operations. The Airmen completed 15,500 missions, destroyed over 260 enemy aircraft, sank one enemy destroyer, and demolished numerous enemy installations. Several aviators died in combat. The Tuskegee Airmen were awarded numerous high honors, including Distinguished Flying Crosses, Legions of Merit, Silver Stars, Purple Hearts, the Croix de Guerre, and the Red Star of Yugoslavia. [. . . .]

The Tuskegee Airmen of the 477th Bombardment Group never saw action in WWII. However, they staged a peaceful, non-violent protest for equal rights at Freeman Field, Indiana, in April 1945.

Their achievements proved conclusively

that the Tuskegee Airmen were highly disciplined and capable fighters. They earned the respect of fellow bomber crews and of military leaders. Having fought America's enemies abroad, the Tuskegee Airmen returned to America to join the struggle to win equality at home. [6]

The Tuskegee Airman program ended in December, 1945. With the war over and an abundant supply of pilots, the military had no further need for the aviation training school at Tuskegee.

Using the G. I. Bill to pay for his schooling, Herb entered North Carolina College at Durham, North Carolina[7] to complete his education. He decided to abandon his plans to become a doctor because he needed to be able to support his family and he couldn't do this while spending all those years in medical school and internships. He changed his major to Business Administration.

Wilhelmina remained in Tuskegee for six

---

[6] National Park Service ParkNet: – The Tuskegee Airmen –Overview: Legends of Tuskegee 3/16/2007 <http://www.cr.nps.gov/museum/exhibits/Tuskegee/aircombat>

months and then she went to Wadesboro to live with her mother and father-in-laws. Her sister, Mildred, and her husband, Russell, stayed in Tuskegee for another two years before moving to Pensacola, Florida. Russell ran a hot dog stand for those two years in Tuskegee. They had one child, Sheila, while living in Tuskegee and three other children were born in Florida. Russell became a representative for the now defunct Ballantine Brewery in Florida.

[7] North Carolina College at Durham became North Carolina Central University in 1969.

Parents: Mr. Charles Flowers, Sr. and his wife, Ola Huntley Flowers, circa 1940.

Cadet. Charles Flowers, Jr., age 23; photo taken in 1941.

In the center is Captain Roy F. Morse, Air Corps, teaching aviation cadets how to send and receive code in January 1942. On the left, from front to rear: James B. Knighten, Lee Rayford, and C.H. Flowers. On the right, from front to rear: George Levi Knox, Sherman W. Whilte, and Mac Ross. From the Air University/HO, Maxwell AFB, Alabama, photo collection.

Aviation cadets at Tuskegee Army Air Field are reviewed by the base commander Maj. James Ellison. Herbert Flowers is the third cadet from the right. (Col. Roosevelt J. Lewis collection at Moton Field).

Lieutenant Donald McPherson, center, explains aspects of a cross country training trip to a croup of cadets. From left: Bernard McKnighten, George Roberts, Sherman White, Herbert Flowers, Sr., George Knox, Lt. McPherson, Lee Rayford, and last three cadets are un-identified; March 1942..

Flight Instructor – Charles Herbert Flowers, left, inspects a plane with cadet, Eugene E. Richardson, Tuskegee Army Air Field, circa 1942.

Civilian flight instructors at Tuskegee Army Air Field: Civilian flight instructors at Tuskegee Army Air Field: Bottom row; left to right – Perry Young, Oberlin, Ohio; Charles H. Flowers, Wadesboro, N.C.: Claude Platt, Forth Worth, Texas; Charles A. Anderson (chief pilot), Bridgeport, Pennsylvania; C.R. Harris, Wilksboro, N.C.; Wendell R. Lipscomb, Berkley, California; James E. Wright, Savannah, Georgia. Top row; left to right: Robert Terry, Greensboro, N.C.; John H. Young III, Pine Bluff, Arkansas; Charles W. Stephens Jr., Monroeville, Alabama; Charles R. Foxx, West Palm Beach Florida; Roscoe D. Draper, Haverford, Pennsylvania; Sherman T. Rose, Jefferson City Missouri; James A. Hill, Oklahoma City, Oklahoma; Adolph J. Moret Jr., New Orleans, Louisiana; Earnest Henderson, Mountville, S.C.; Matthew W. Plummer, San Antonio, Texas; Linkwood Williams, Madison, Illinois; Daniel James, Pensacola, Florida; Lewis A. Jackson, Argola, Indiana, and Milton P. Crenchaw, Little Rock, Arkansas. Photographed by Major Roosevelt Montgomery.

FINAL ACTION ON BOU

Mass Challenges Th

EX-ARMY ACE C. H. Flowers, Jr., of Durham, former officer in the famous 99th Pursuit squadron which served in Italy, will participate in the all-Negro air show at Plaza airport Saturday and Sunday, performing precision acrobatic flying.

Just For Laughs

'Pants' Race To Be Staged At Air Show

No show is complete without a vein of humor, and the promoter of the all-Negro Air carnival at Plaza Airport next Saturday and Sunday has worked out a set of events that will put the customers in stitches.

Haskell A. Deaton, promoting the big two-day show for the benefit of the building funds of the Charlotte Negro Y. M. C. A. and Y. W. C. A., announced last night that a "pants" race involving three pilots will be one of the fun-producers. Here's how it works. The three

FLOODLIGHTING CONTRACT LET

Athletic Areas at Freedom

ELECTION BODY ASKED TO PURGE BALLOT BOOKS

Former County Republican Leader Demands Complete New Registration Before Next Primary.

BY PORTER MUNN
Observer Staff Writer.

E. J. Presser, former chairman of the Mecklenburg county Republican executive committee, last night issued a blasting threat that if the Mecklenburg election board fails to have a complete new registration before the registration period preceding the general primary next spring, challenges against allegedly ineligible voters can be expected by the thousands.

Mr. Presser is the moving force behind the recent series of challenges which were registered in Ward 7, Box 3, and Ward 8, Box 3. He was assisted in the challenging by Robert W. Alexander, head of the Mecklenburg Young Republican club.

IN EXPLAINING the protests against allegedly ineligible voters at this time, just before the June 14 ABC vote, Mr. Presser said that this election was selected for the challenges because the election is nonpartisan.

He said that the need for a new registration is vital to insure genuine representation of the people at the polls. He explained that

Charles Herbert Flowers, Jr. is pictured in the Charlotte Observer after performing aerobatics during an air show that featured black pilots in July of 1947.

Charles. and Wilhelmina Flowers are shown with other family members at the funeral of his maternal grandfather in Wadesboro, NC in 1947. Front row from left, his Aunt Beaulah, his father, his mother, Charles Flowers, Jr., Wilhelmina Flowers, an aunt, Leona. 2nd Row: An uncle, his uncle, Tom, an un-identified lady, and un-identified gentleman, his Aunt Anna Belle, his Aunt Ailene, Uncle Robert. 3rd Row: Another Uncle Tom, his father-in-law, Aunt Jeullia, Uncle Lislie, Uncle J.P., un-identified lady, Step-aunt Maguerita, Step-uncle Odell Leeks.

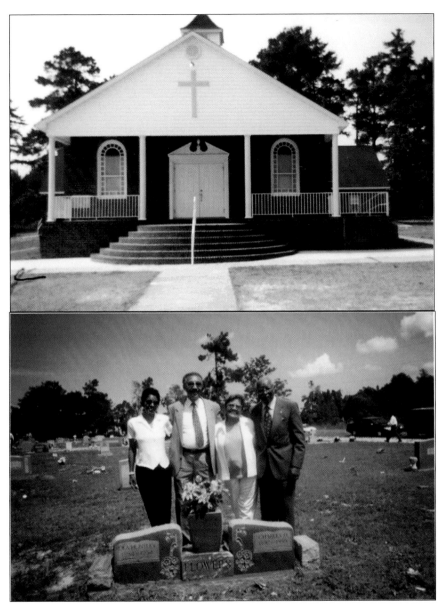

Top: A recent photo of Gateway Station African Methodist Episcopal
(AME) Zion church. Below: Daughter Carolyn Flowers Green, Son-in-Law
Alvin Green, Wife Mrs. Wilhelmina Flowers and Mr. Charles Flowers at the
graves of his parents. Mrs. Ola Flowers, his mother, became the first person
to be buried in the cemetery that she was very instrumental in establishing.

Wilhelmina and Charles Herbert Flowers, Jr.

Herbert Flowers shown with some of his NAI students in 1997.

Orientation day – Mentors Flying Program. Herbert Flowers is shown 4th from left.

Maryland General Assembly honoring Charles Flowers during Black History Month; February 27, 1997. Left to Right: Maryland State Senator Nathaniel Exum, Spealer of Maryland House of Delegates – Casper Taylor, Charles H. Flowers Maryland State Delegate – Joanne C. Benson and Maryland State Delegate Carolyn J.B. Howard

Members of the East Coast Chapter of Tuskegee Airmen, Inc. pose in front of Charles Herbert Flowers, Jr. High School during its dedication.

Charles Herbert Flowers, Jr. is shown in front of an AT-6, also known as the Advanced Trainer and the Texan. He has more than 100 hours of flight in this plane. Photo by Harriett Smith.

Nearly 300 Tuskegee Airmen attended their Congressional Gold Medal ceremony on March 29, 2007 in Statuary Hall of the U.S. Capitol. Photo – courtesy White House Photography Office, photo by Joyce Boghosian. President George W. Bush and Speaker of the House of Representatives – Nancy Pilosi – are both shown side-by-side in center of photo..

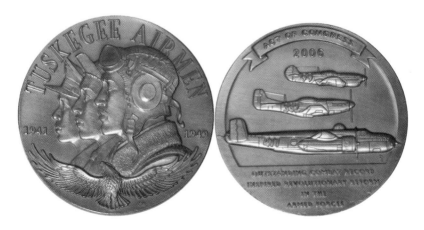

Photo of the Congressional Gold Medal awarded to Charles Flowers. on March 29, 2007.

Charles Herbert Flowers receives "Man of the Year Award" at Ebenezer United Methodist Church, November 9, 2008. From Left to Right: Reverend Adamio Charles Boddie (Men's Day speaker), Charles Flowers, Wilhelmina Flowers, and Reverend Mark D. Venson – Pastor of Ebenezer United Methodist Church.

February 23, 2006. Photo shows Herbert Flowers shown in his cap and gown, and with his Honorary Doctorate in Public Service at Tuskegee University.

College, Careers and Family Life in North Carolina

Herb entered North Carolina College (N.C.C.) at Durham, now North Carolina Central University, in January 1946. His and Wilhelmina's second child, Yvonne, was born in Monroe, North Carolina and delivered by Wilhelmina's brother-in-law, Dr. Hubert Creft, on February 23, 1946. Herb rented a house on Linwood Avenue in Durham from which to begin their new life. Then he rented a truck and drove back to Tuskegee to move their furniture to the house in Durham. Wilhelmina, Carolyn, and Yvonne then moved to Durham to be with Herb.

With his family settled in Durham, Herb buckled down to the business of completing his college education. He continued to excel in his classes and he was active in campus organizations and student affairs. He joined a fraternity, Omega Psi Phi, a black fraternity that dates back to 1911. N.C.C. did not have a Student Government Association. During the last junior class meeting of his junior year, the junior class decided that they wanted to do something as a tribute to North Carolina College. Herb suggested that they start a Student Government Association. Herb attended summer school that year and during that time he was appointed as chairman of the committee to write a constitution and bylaws for the SGA. Herb ran against Harold Epps (a member of Alpha Phi Alpha, the oldest Greek-letter fraternity established for blacks in 1906) for the presidency of the SGA; it made for a nice, friendly fraternal rivalry. In the fall of 1946, Herb was elected as the first president of the N.C.C. Student Government Association. The following year, Herb was also elected Vice President of the Senior Class. Herb graduated in June 1947. All of his family attended his graduation and they were very proud of him.

After graduation, Herb got a job in Charlotte, North Carolina for the Haskell Deaton Flying Service which belonged to a gentleman by the name of Haskell Deaton, a white man. In July 1947, the flying service had an air show featuring Negro pilots. Herb was invited to participate along with Charlie Fox, another flight instructor from Tuskegee. Herb flew a glider plane in the show. This was the first time that Herb had ever flown a glider (a plane with no engine).

Wilhelmina participated in the Charlotte Air Show as well. She took the controls and flew a plane while in the air. The white couple with her was sitting in the seat in back of her (the husband was the actual pilot). A photographer, from one of the leading Black Newspapers of that time, took a picture of her standing beside the airplane and the paper ran an article about this event entitled "Black Woman Carries Up White Couple." Her father was so proud of his daughter that he carried that picture around with him and showed it to all his friends. This all-Negro Air show was described in the Charlotte Observer as a two man, one woman show.

Herb also participated in another air show sometime later in Greensboro along with Robert Terry, another Tuskegee Airman Flight Instructor. These air shows gave Black pilots an avenue by which they could show off their flying skills.

Haskell Deaton and Herb formed a partnership to open a flying school to teach servicemen to fly using the G. I. Bill. Herb taught the blacks and Haskell taught the whites. This partnership lasted about six months (July 1947 – February 1948) because the Veterans Administration (VA) began requiring veterans to show where they would be employed as pilots before paying for flight training.

Black pilots were not being hired by any commercial airlines at that time due to racial discrimination so Black veterans could not receive money for pilot training based on that new requirement.

With their flying skills not useful for civilian employment, some Tuskegee Airmen stayed in the military and others used the G. I. bill to attend school to prepare for other careers. Once, after graduating from college, Herb ran into one of the former white Tuskegee flight instructors, Forest Shelton. Forest told him that Piedmont Airlines needed pilots and encouraged him to apply. Herb went to Piedmont to apply and the airline personnel manager took one look at him and said that he couldn't hire him because his stockholders would go crazy. This sort of thing happened again and again to black men who were trained to be pilots and had served in the military during the war. [8]

During the time that he was associated with Haskell Deaton, Herb began looking for another house to buy for his family. He looked in Charlotte and Durham but could not find the house that he wanted. His association with Haskell Deaton gave him access to planes, so he took a flight over the state looking for a house to buy. He flew over

---

[8] Commercial Airlines did not begin hiring African American pilots until 1965.

Winston-Salem and found a new housing development being built for Blacks. He found a house that he liked there. He took Wilhelmina by plane to look at the house and they decided to buy in that development even though Herb did not have a job in Winston-Salem.

While Herb was a flight instructor at Tuskegee, he had taken a two-year evening course titled, "The Design and Operation of Radios and Electronics," in the Tuskegee Institute Department of Engineering and Electronics. After he completed the course, he became a certified electronics technician. This training plus his college Bachelor of Science degree in Business Administration opened the door to a new job opportunity once the family moved to Winston-Salem. One of his new neighbors, a lawyer named Curtis Todd who lived across the street, owned the Dell Watts Radio Institute, a school which offered training in radio and TV repair to young Black men. Herb got a job teaching radio electronics, physics and math at this school. He taught there from 1948 to 1950.

Herb and Wilhelmina joined Goler Memorial AME Zion Church of Winston-Salem. Herb and Wilhelmina and all the children attended church and Sunday school regularly and were faithful members. Church was an important part of the Flowers' family life.

In 1950, the city of Winston-Salem voted to

open up Alcoholic Beverage Control (ABC) stores. The city had been dry until that time. Herb was one of two blacks hired to manage one of the ABC stores. He gave up teaching to take this job because it paid more money. Several public school teachers also quit teaching to work at the ABC stores because of the greater salary. The Alcoholic Beverage Control Store was for the legal sale of alcoholic beverages. There were six clerks and one utility worker on Herb's staff. The store was located in an all black neighborhood on East 5th Street. It was open from 9 am to 9 pm six days a week. It closed on Sundays. A booming business was done in these stores and the revenue went to the city. Strict rules governed the sale of this alcohol. You could not sell to anyone who appeared to be under the influence of alcohol at the time of purchase and you could not sell to anyone underage. Public drinking was against the law. So purchasers had to take their alcohol home unopened or risk being arrested.

Herb worked at the ABC store from 1950 – 1959. During these years, his family grew to four children. Their third child, Charles Herbert Flowers, III (Herbie) was born August 10, 1950. Roderick Dean Flowers was born June 10, 1954. He was born just after Herb's mother died in May 1954.

Ola Flowers passed away suddenly of a cerebral hemorrhage at the age of 59 and on the last day of school. Herb had just wired flowers to her for

Mother's day. She was in her classroom when she died. She had taught school for over 35 years. In 1950, Ola had been able to persuade the church leadership to purchase land adjacent to the Gatewood Station AME Zion Church which would be used as the church cemetery. Prior to doing this, burials of church members were done in a cemetery which belonged to a Baptist Church located four miles away. Ola became the first person to be buried in the church cemetery which she had been so instrumental in establishing. (The church is still in existence along with the cemetery. The church structure has been rebuilt and the cemetery is almost full today.)

In March 1955, Herb joined the Masons. He became a member of James H. Young Memorial Lodge #670. He was an active member in the Lodge for the remainder of the time that he lived in Winston-Salem.

Herb quit the ABC Store position in 1959 when he and Wilhelmina decided to go into the drug store business. Dr. John Quick, Sr. owned a drug store in downtown Winston-Salem. It was being run by his son, Dr. John Quick, Jr., a pharmacist. The business was not doing well under the son, so the father decided to sell it. Herb heard about this. He was ready to leave the ABC store manager job because there wasn't much of a future in it for him since it gave him no chance for advancement. So he and his brother-in-law, Dr. Perry P. Little from High Point N.C., formed a partnership to buy the drug store business (not the building). Dr. Quick owned the building and had his office on the second floor. The drugstore was in a good location. It was on a busy downtown street with a bus stop outside the store. They changed the name from Atlantic Pharmacy to Church Street Pharmacy.

Herb and Wilhelmina operated and managed the store. It sold ice cream, magazines, household items, and other things along with prescription drugs. Wilhelmina worked part time in the pharmacy, taking and dispensing prescriptions for customers. Carolyn and Yvonne worked in the store after school. It was a family business. The drug store was very profitable during the three years that they owned it. They had to close the store when Winston-Salem's urban renewal activities resulted in the business being bought out along with all the old buildings in that part of town. The area was redeveloped with high rises and fancy shops.

All of the Flowers children had attended elementary school in Winston-Salem. The school system was a good one even though it was segregated. Carolyn and Yvonne finished Atkins High School in Winston-Salem. Carolyn was a B plus student and a cheerleader. Yvonne was the Valedictorian of her class. Winston-Salem was home for them. So, it was undoubtedly hard for them to leave when the family decided to move to Glenarden, Maryland after the Drug Store was closed.

Chapter 7

Life in Glenarden, Maryland

During the time that he owned his drug store business, Herb learned about job opportunities at Goddard Space Flight Center in Greenbelt, Maryland from Dr. John Quick, Jr., the drug store pharmacist. Dr. Quick had attended pharmacy school at Howard University and was familiar with the job market in the Washington, DC area. Goddard which today has the largest collection of scientist and engineers involved with understanding the "earth, the solar system and universe," was established as NASA's first flight control center in 1959 with NASA (National Aeronautics and Space Administration) having been founded in 1958.

Herb's industriousness in attending night school classes in electronics while at Tuskegee paid off once more. In 1962 Herb applied for a job with

Computer Sciences Corporation (CSC) as an electronic technician. CSC was one of the largest civilian government contractors in the area and they offered him the job. He rented a room for a year from a senior widow, Ms. Melby, while the rest of his family remained in Winston-Salem.

He bought the family's current home in Glenarden in 1963. He had been able to watch his new home being built. It was in a middle class neighborhood of hard working, professional African American families and is approximately 10 miles from Washington, D.C.

After Yvonne graduated from Atkins High School in Winston-Salem in 1964, the family moved to their new home in Glenarden. By this time, Carolyn was attending North Carolina College at Durham, her father's Alma Mata. Yvonne got a job at Goddard, so that she could work and save money for college. Charles, III began middle school and Roderick entered elementary school in the Prince Georges county school system. Wilhelmina opened up a beauty shop in the basement which she would operate for the next three years.

Herb stayed in the electronic technician position for a year and a half. Then he advanced to a new position as Satellite Missions Operation Control Coordinator. This job involved controlling satellites from the ground.

Carolyn surprised her parents by marrying her

high school sweetheart, Alvin Green, in 1965. She left college and moved to Winston-Salem to be with her husband. Yvonne, in the mean time, had enrolled in North Carolina College to continue her education. But in 1967, Yvonne followed in her sister's foot steps once more. She married her high school sweetheart, John Chester Hinton, and moved to Winston-Salem, too. So, both sisters were back in the town where they had grown up. Both girls were beauties with wonderful personalities like their mother, Wilhelmina. Carolyn had been elected Miss Sophomore and Yvonne had been elected Miss Freshman while attending NCC. Those young men were not going to let the Flowers' sisters get away.

In 1967, Herb advanced to the position of scientific computer programmer/analyst. He programmed in FORTRAN, PL1, and Autocoder on IBM computers (1410, 7010, 360). Advancement would continue for him; in 1972, Herb became the Employee Relations Manager for CSC. He managed a branch of three employees. They handled personnel problems for CSC, primarily discrimination complaints. His branch handled problems for all the 800 employees of the Defense Systems Division of CSC.

About that same time, Wilhelmina, who had been attending Prince Georges Community College received a certificate for Early Childhood Development. Upon receiving her certification she opened a licensed day care center in the basement of their home. She was industrious and always seeking ways to make additional income for the family.

The Flowers family was a close knit family. Herb and Wilhelmina encouraged their children to succeed, applauding all their accomplishments and supporting them when they chose different paths contrary to their wishes. Charles, III (Herbie) played football for Du Val High School in Prince Georges. He was a good student and after he graduated from Du Val in 1968, he was accepted for admission by Morgan State University and the Air Force Academy. To his parent's great disappointment, he did not want to go to college. He chose, instead, to marry Gail Marbly, his sweetheart, who lived in the same neighborhood as the Flowers. They had one son. Herbie attended drafting school after the marriage ended. He is a talented artist who has painted family portraits which adorn his parents' walls in their home. After his first wife, Gail, passed away, years later, he married Andrea Sedgwick and they had one son.

Herb and Wilhelmina's son Roderick was placed in the Talented and Gifted program and attended Pullen Junior High School in Prince Georges. He was good in art and liked to design clothes. At the age of twelve, he was interviewed by NBC news and written up in the Washington Post as the Designer of the Year. He had many fashion shows in schools and churches. One of his classmates, Janet Armstrong, was his seamstress.

In 1973, Roderick graduated from Du Val High School. He entered the Parsons School of Art in New York. Upon completion of art school, he pursued his career in the fashion world in New York. While in New York, Roderick did not take care of his health. In 1988, he became deathly ill and had to return to his parents' home in Glenarden. They cared for him as best as they could, but in July 1988, he passed away. Wilhelmina took his death very hard.

In the early 1970's, Wilhelmina had begun to work outside of the home. First, she worked as the senior teacher at Addison Day Care in Seat Pleasant, Maryland. Then she worked at the Early Childhood training School in Glenarden, Maryland. To cope with her great loss after the death of her son, she enrolled in Bible College. In 1988, at the same time that she was attending Bible College, Wilhelmina started working as the Manager of the Senior Citizens Center in New Carrollton, Maryland. She loved working with the seniors and helping them with their problems. This job was a ministry for her.

Carolyn shared her father's love for flying and this led her to seek employment in the airline industry. Carolyn worked for Eastern Airlines in North Carolina from 1968 to 1989 as a reservation agent. This enabled her to get cheap flights for family members and the Flowers' family, who loved to fly, took full advantage of this perk. Currently, Carolyn and her husband manage two Allstate Insurance Offices in Charlotte, North Carolina. Carolyn has three children and she is the grandmother of six.

In 1989, after 27 years at CSC, Herb retired. That didn't mean he went home to his rocking chair. He looked for something else to do and found a job with H&R block on Minnesota Avenue Northeast, Washington, D. C. from January to April 15 of each year. At one time, He was offered a management position at the Rhode Island Avenue office in DC but Herb was not interested in another management job.

In 1991, Wilhelmina completed two years of training at the Jericho Christian Training College in Washington, D. C. Her studies were in biblical theology and healing. She took her healing course under Charles and Francis Hunter. She graduated with honors. Wilhelmina has had many religious experiences. She, herself, has been healed and she has prayed for the healing of others: family members, friends and neighbors.

Tragedy struck the Flowers family once more in 1992. Their youngest daughter, Beatrice Yvonne, was diagnosed with advanced colon cancer. At that time, she was the Vice President of Wachovia Bank in Winston-Salem. She passed away on New Year's

Day in 1993 just a short time after her diagnosis. Yvonne was the mother of one son. Her son graduated from A&T in Greensboro with honors and has one child.

Thru all their trials and challenging times, Herb and Wilhelmina held to their religious faith. They were always connected to the church, no matter where they lived. After they were settled in Glenarden, they attended a Baptist Church but Herb decided not to join because this church required an immersion baptism, and Herb had already been baptized by sprinkling and did not feel that it was necessary to be "dunked" in the water. Wilhelmina went to Glenarden Baptist for a while. Herb joined Ebenezer United Methodist Church in Lanham, Maryland. Wilhelmina joined as well. The minister at that time was Reverend Crider.

Herb has been a very active member of Ebenezer: Church Treasurer (1975-1981), Usher Board, Men's Ensemble, Pastor Parrish Relations Committee, United Methodist Men, Liturgist, and Edward L. Williams Mentoring Program. Wilhelmina left Ebenezer after Reverend Conrad Parker left. He was a spirit filled, charismatic minister. Many members, who were disappointed about his leaving, left for other churches as well. Wilhelmina joined Jericho Baptist Church of Washington, D. C. around 1990. And she has been a member of the Missionary Club of Jericho through the years.

Training the Best

Herb was never interested in politics. He attended a few town hall meetings for the city of Glenarden. Once, he was encouraged by a friend to run for Mayor but, of course, he said, "No thanks." State Senator Tommie Broadwater was a neighbor of the Flowers' family. Herb once asked Senator Broadwater if he would like to take flying lessons. The Senator didn't know what to think of that query. At the time, he didn't realize what Herb's background was. As a matter of fact, none of the Flowers' neighbors knew what a significant role Herb had played in American history.

Herb finally retired from the H&R Block job in 2005. He needed to slow down. Due to health problems, Wilhelmina had to retire from the Senior Center job in 2005 after working there for 17 years. They both have worked diligently and faithfully all their lives, enriching all those that they touched.

Herb's Aviation Activities in Glenarden

Herb became a member of The East Coast Chapter of the Tuskegee Airmen, Inc. (TAI) shortly after it was formed. The East Coast Chapter is the oldest chapter of TAI. It was incorporated in Washington, D. C. in 1972. The group initially consisted of about 15 of the original pilots but later expanded to become an umbrella group for all persons who were involved in the Tuskegee Aviation program between the years of 1941 and 1946. Some of the other original members were Spann Watson, Gordon Southall, and William Broadwater.

The East Coast chapter was formed almost forty years ago by a group in the Washington, D.C. metropolitan area after a few preliminary meetings were held with Tuskegee Airmen in other parts of the country – notably, Detroit, Michigan. It was 1972 when someone came up with the idea of getting together all of the guys who were former Tuskegee Airmen. Letters were sent to all the former Tuskegee pilots all over the country, suggesting they meet in Detroit. Three former Airmen from Washington, D.C., went to the Detroit meeting: John Suggs, Eldridge Jackson and Willie Ashley. Ashley was one of the original Tuskegee Airmen who went over to Italy with Colonel Benjamin O. Davis, Jr. as a member of the first group of pilots to head to war. That meeting in Detroit marked the beginning of formal efforts to create an organization.

The affair was a good start, but more work was required. Meeting participants asked Suggs to see if he could begin an organization in Washington, D.C. So upon his return to Washington, Suggs and Eldridge Jackson sent letters to all of the Tuskegee Airmen they knew in the area suggesting a meeting at a local church. About thirty people responded, and the Tuskegee Airmen, Inc. was established. Officers elected at that first meeting were: John Suggs - President or commander; Kenny White - Vice President; Harry Shepherd – Secretary and Curtis Robinson, Treasurer. William Broadwater was the head of the board. These men got the organization operating and decided to have the first nationwide convention in Washington, D.C. They formalized the organizational structure - got their 501(c)(3) and 501 (c)(19) designations from the government - raised money, sent out invitations to every Tuskegee Airman they could think of, planned and held the first Tuskegee Airmen, Inc. convention.

Their convention, held on August 10th – 12th of 1973, was very well attended, extremely successful and was an auspicious beginning for the group. They divided the country into three regions; East Coast, West Coast, and Central, although there were to be numerous chapters within these regions. Detroit, Chicago, Denver, and Kansas City, for example, would be part of the Central region; Philadelphia, Washington, Atlanta, and New York would be East Coast. The West Coast included Los Angeles, San Francisco, Sacramento, plus a few other cities. Spann Watson became president of the national chapter and under his leadership, the national organization received its 501(c)(3) designation on February 21, 1975. The registered address was Washington, D.C., though today it is Arlington, VA.

Since that time, the organization has opened up to all who are interested in aviation. There are over 50 chapters in this country and overseas. Today, the East Coast Chapter consists of Maryland, D. C., Virginia and North Carolina.

The primary goal of the organization is to inspire young people to excel in all of their endeavors as well as to inform them and the general public of the "Tuskegee Experience." Today, organizational membership is open to the public. This group wants to encourage young people to become aviators but is not limited to that field. The mission statement for Tuskegee Airmen, Inc. is:

> To bring together in a spirit of friendship and goodwill all persons who share in the aspirations and successes of the men and women who pioneered in military aviation and in the Tuskegee experience, to foster recognition of and preserve the history of Black achievements in aviation, and to inspire and motivate young men and women toward endeavors in aviation and aerospace careers.[9]

Herb Flowers, Jr. has been an active and faithful member since joining. He attends meetings, accepts speaking engagements on behalf of the organization and attends as many events featuring the Airmen as he possibly can.

Between 1974 and 1981, Herb was hired to be the flight instructor for the Howard University Flying Club. On the weekends, Herb taught students to fly. He was recruited for this position by Dr. Arthur Thorpe, a military pilot, who was trained after the Tuskegee Aviation program ended.

---

[9] East Coast Chapter Tuskegee Airmen, Inc: 4/9/2007

<http://www.ecctai.com/ecc/ecchistory.htm>

Herb's Aviation Activities in Glenarden

In 1989 Herb was approached by Negro Airmen International, Inc (NAI) and asked to become a flight instructor in their Summer Flight Academy. The NAI paid Herb's travel and lodging expenses, but Herb's flight instruction was voluntary work. This was a two-week flight training program for students held in Tuskegee, Alabama in July of each year. Herb was a flight instructor in this program from 1989 to 1997, giving 10 hours of flight instruction to four or five students for two weeks. Some of his students actually soloed during those two weeks.

The Negro Airmen International, Inc. (NAI) is the oldest black civilian aviation group in the world. It was founded in February 1967 by Edward A. Gibbs and several of the Tuskegee Airmen instructors. (Mr. Gibbs completed the CPT Program at Hampton Institute (now Hampton University) and was a flight instructor at Schumaker Flying Service and taught navigation and regulations at the Coffey School of Aviation.) NAI, Inc was founded to "help Americans of African decent to learn about the field of aviation, to create job opportunities, and to encourage more Blacks to go into the field of aviation."[10]

In 1996, William Broadwater, the then

---

[10] Negro Airmen International, Inc. (NAI) : 9/3/2007
<http://www.blackwings.com/about.html>

President of the East Coast Chapter of Tuskegee Airmen, Inc., asked Herb and Theodore Robinson, another original Tuskegee Airman, to form a committee to develop an aviation training program for youth. Their committee developed the "Youth in Aviation Program," which is still in existence today. (Yvonne McGee and Nelson Evans are currently in charge of the program.) In the program, high school students are introduced to various aviation careers: Aircraft Mechanics, Air Traffic Controllers, Pilots, etc. Student pilots receive 15 hours of flight training which is paid for by the chapter. Very few take advantage of this phase of the training. It may have something to do with a general fear of flying. Flight orientation is held at College Park Airport. Ground and flight training is held at Hyde Field in Clinton, Maryland. For many years, this facility was owned and operated by Herbert H. Jones, a member of the East Coast Chapter of the Tuskegee Airmen, Inc. He joined the chapter after 1980.

Herb has been a member of the Edward L. Williams Mentoring Program since its inception in 1990. He has been instrumental in setting up and coordinating its annual "Flight Orientation Day." On that day, the mentors and the protégées take a bus to Hyde Airfield where the protégées experience flying a small aircraft under the guidance of an experienced pilot. During the early years of this activity, Herb was one of the pilots who took the boys up for a flight. Even though he still has a pilot's license, Herb stopped flying in his mid eighties because he felt that his reflexes had slowed too much to continue flying.

Training the Best

Chapter 9

Charles Herbert Flowers High School

In 1989, Boyd and Dorothy Poole joined Ebenezer United Methodist Church. It was a joyful church with a great choir, a dynamic preacher, and a friendly congregation. They discovered that the distinguished looking usher, Herb Flowers, was an original Tuskegee Airman. When Boyd became superintendent of the Sunday school, he assumed responsibility for the upstairs bulletin board. For Black History Month, Dorothy decided that it would be a great idea to put up a bulletin board featuring Mr. Flowers and the Tuskegee Airmen. She called Mrs. Flowers and asked for and received pictures and articles about Mr. Flowers and the Tuskegee Airmen.

Boyd joined the United Methodists Men's group and became acquainted with Mr. Flowers. He discovered that Mr. Flowers was a wonderful and humble person thru his involvement in the Mentoring Program that was established by the Men's group. Mr. Flowers was a dedicated mentor who was loved by parents and students alike. Boyd was working for State Delegate Nathaniel Exum of the 24th Legislative District of Maryland at the time.[11] In February 1997, he suggested to Delegate Exum that the General Assembly honor Mr. Flowers for Black History Month. Plans were put into action by Delegate Exum.

On Friday, February 27, 1997, the General Assembly honored Mr. Flowers as an African American Hero. This event was inspiring to all who attended.

In September, 1997, Delegate Exum was at the United Methodist's Men's Prayer breakfast, and Boyd expressed a desire to him to further honor Mr. Flowers and the Tuskegee Airmen Flight Instructors. He asked if it would be possible to name a school after Mr. Flowers as an honor to the Tuskegee Airmen and their Flight Instructors. Delegate Exum replied in the affirmative. Boyd established a committee to accomplish this goal: "The Committee to Honor the Tuskegee Airmen Flight Instructors

---

[11] State Delegate Nathaniel Exum of the 24th Legislative District was elected to the Maryland State Senate in 1998. At the time of the naming of the high school in honor of Charles Herbert Flowers, Jr., Mr. Exum was State Senator Exum of the 24th Legislative District.

and Specifically Aviation Cadet Captain Charles Herbert Flowers."

This committee asked for and received the support of over a hundred Maryland civic, religious and political leaders. It sent a proposal for the naming of the new science and technical high school being built in Springdale, Maryland to Kenneth E. Johnson, the Chairman of the Prince Georges County School Board. Mr. Johnson took the matter of the naming of the school before the board and other civic groups.

Some civic groups had other names in mind for the school. Some members of the Springdale community, where the school would be located, wanted the school to be named Springdale Senior High School while others wanted the school to be named for deceased local civic leaders. There arose quite a controversy over the naming of the school. Articles appeared in the local newspaper, the Gazette, which were pro and con about the naming of a school after a person who was still alive. Generally, schools were named for deceased individuals but that rule could be waived. It was not unprecedented to have buildings named for individuals still living.

Many people in the community were unaware of Mr. Flowers' background and spread rumors that he was not a Tuskegee Airman and not a pilot. They believed that the only Tuskegee Airmen were the ones who flew combat missions during World War

II. They were quite unaware of the facts surrounding the Tuskegee Airmen Program and the diverse makeup of the program's members.

To counter all the false rumors and misperceptions, the East Coast Chapter of the Tuskegee Airmen, Inc. gave Mr. Flowers their complete support. They wrote letters and testified on his behalf at school board hearings. Boyd and Dorothy Poole compiled a document with pictures and newspaper articles on Mr. Flowers from his days as a Tuskegee Airman and Flight Instructor. This document was sent to Kenneth Johnson's assistant, Patti Knick. She made color copies of the document and gave one to each School Board Member on the night that the vote for the naming of the school was to be held. This document dispelled all the false rumors about Mr. Flowers not being an original Tuskegee Airman. Kenneth Johnson threw his full support behind naming the school "Charles Herbert Flowers High School." School Superintendent Iris T. Metts also gave her full support to the Flowers school name. All other board member concurred and the vote in favor was unanimous.

On Saturday August 26, 2000, the school was officially dedicated as "Charles Herbert Flowers High School." The school auditorium was packed with school officials, politicians, members of the East Coast Chapter of the Tuskegee Airmen, Inc., students and parents and other well wishers.

Charles Herbert Flowers High School

The new principal of Flowers High School, Helena Nobles-Jones, was delighted to have her school's name sake alive and well and more than willing to be a role model for the students.

The school's name took on real meaning because the students had Mr. Flowers to listen to and to emulate. Mr. Flowers has made himself available to attend many student functions held at the school. The students love him and he loves them. He continuously advises students on the value of a good education as his parents had advised him.

About a year after the school opened, Boyd asked William Holton, Historian for the East Coast Chapter of the Tuskegee Airmen, to create a display on the Tuskegee Airmen and Mr. Flowers and the Civilian Flight Instructors for Flowers High School. Mr. Holton commissioned an artist to make the drawings and Boyd made requests for donations from local politicians to finance this project. The display was placed on the walls of the rear entrance of Charles Herbert Flowers High School for all to see and read and learn about the Tuskegee Airmen and their Flight Instructors.

Training the Best

Local and National Honors

On Saturday, February 11, 2006, Charles Herbert Flowers was honored by the Wadesboro Branch of The National Association of University Women and The Gatewood Station AME Zion church, (Charles, Sr. and Ola Flower's family church). Herb, Wilhelmina and other family members attended. The other special guests were North Carolina House of Representative Pryor Gibson, Anson County Sheriff Tommy Woodburn, and Chairman of the Anson County Board of Commissioners, Mr. Jarvis Woodburn. There were speeches and presentations given, and solos sung. Herb's home town folk wanted him to know how special he was to them. This was also an opportunity for the young people in the church to see their hometown hero and learn of his contributions toward making this a better world.

On February 23, 2006, Tuskegee University awarded all pilots who completed training in the Army Air Corps Flight School between 1941 and 1946 honorary doctorates in public service. There were forty-seven pilots at Tuskegee to receive their awards. Herb was one of the forty-seven there to receive his Honorary Doctorate Degree in Public Service.

At the time of the Gatewood Station program, no one in Wadesboro knew that their own Charles Herbert Flowers, Jr. would be receiving an even greater honor. On Thursday, March 29, 2007, all the surviving Tuskegee Airmen were honored by the United States Congress with a Congressional Gold Medal of Honor.

Those who were honored were those who trained in and/or served the Tuskegee Aviation Program and Army Air Corps training at Tuskegee, Alabama between 1941 and 1946. It was a long overdue honor. These men and women served their country well, dispelling myths about the intelligence and fitness of African Americans to fly and serve in other challenging duties in the military.

> More than 10,000 African-American men and women in military and civilian groups supported the Tuskegee Airmen. They served as flight instructors, officers,

bombardiers, navigators, radio technicians, mechanics, air traffic controllers, parachute riggers, and electrical and communications specialists.

Support personnel also included laboratory assistants, cooks, musicians, and supply, firefighting, and transportation personnel. Their participation helped pave the way for desegregation of the military that began with President Harry S. Truman's Executive Order 9981 in 1948. The civilian world gradually began to integrate and African Americans entered commercial aviation and the space program.[12]

[12]National Park Service ParkNet: 3/16/2007

<http://www.cr.nps.gov/museum/Tuskegee/airsupport.htm>

The Tuskegee Airmen

The Tuskegee Airmen are the men who trained to be Army Air Corps pilots in Tuskegee, Alabama between 1941 and 1946, and the men and women who supported them. For every pilot trained at Tuskegee, there were about ten support personnel. There were 994 pilots and an additional support staff of approximately 10,000 personnel.

Their experience is often referred to as "The Tuskegee Experience" and it resulted from the attitudes, policies, and practices that existed in America at that the time. It was a time when race relations in the nation were poor, segregation was prevalent, and policies that relegated blacks to low positions in the armed services were widely used.

After World War I, the Army War College had issued studies about the suitability of blacks for serving in the military. Twice, once in 1925 and again in 1937, the War Department commissioned studies that concluded that blacks were cowards, not as smart as whites, and did not have the courage to fight in battle. The study went on to comment on black brain sizes, reasoning ability, and other factors working against them and contained many other very negative conclusions. Those studies formed the basis for the Army Air Corps policy of refusing to accept blacks.

Obviously those studies were false. From early into the 20th century, Black Americans had been very involved with aviation. Several aviation milestones were met by Blacks in the first quarter of the century: Eugene Jacques Bullard, born in Columbus, Georgia, was the only black pilot of World War I. Since blacks were not permitted to fly for the United States at that time, he flew for France's Lafayette Flying Corps from 1914 -1918. Bessie Coleman graduated from the Caudron Flying School in France in June 1921 and received her license there and was the first Black woman to make a public flight in the United States. During the 1920s and 30s, several Black flying clubs were in operation in America, and African-American men and women were receiving licenses as pilots. In October 1932, James H. Banning and Thomas C. Allen became the first African- Americans to make a transcontinental flight.

Moreover, various groups, organizations and factors within the nation were acting to challenge and change the mindset that African-Americans could not fly sophisticated aircraft and to expand opportunities for blacks in the Army Air Corps: First, there were civil right organizations at work – the NAACP, National urban League and the Brotherhood of Sleeping Car Porters - fighting for change; next, black newspapers – Pittsburgh Courier, the Afro, and the Norfolk Journal and Guide were pressing the issue; the presidential election of 1940 involved leveraging the issue, a lawsuit filed by a college student against the War Department added additional heat, war preparation for World War II, and common sense were all converging to change things.

In December 1940, the War Department submitted a plan for an "experiment" involving black pilots. But the Army Air Corps still refused applications from blacks until Yancey Williams, a Howard University college student, filed a suit through the NAACP in 1941. Finally, early in 1941, the War Department announced that blacks would be called into service in proportion to their percentage of the population and an all-black squadron, the 99th Fighter Squadron, would be activated.

By February 1941, Tuskegee Institute had received certification to provide advanced flying courses and would soon receive $1.7 million for an air field. In March 1941, the Selective Service Headquarters said in part, "The Negro pilots will be trained at Tuskegee, Alabama, in connection with

Tuskegee Institute…" Shortly thereafter a training center was established there.

When speaking with the Pittsburgh Courier, once the nation's most widely distributed black newspaper, during the spring of 1941 about the Tuskegee Pilot project and what considerations blacks should use for choosing candidates for the program, Major General Waller R. Weaver, the commander of the Army's Southeastern Air Corps Training Command, pleaded: "For God's sake, send us your best men…For their sake and for our sake, give us your best."

But for the most part, those developments were unbeknownst to the, young black men who had begun their procession to Tuskegee, Alabama to become cadets in the Army Air Corps. The men who arrived as cadets had come from all over the United States and from universities big and small – UCLA, University of Chicago, Arizona State University, McCall University in Canada, Hampton Institute, Howard University, A&T University and many others. Some joined the Army Air Corps at Tuskegee because they truly wanted to fly. Often they came simply seeking better opportunities and pay available in the Army Air Corps than was available in the other branches of military service, and to fulfill their military obligations.

The first class of cadets would enter the program in June of 1941 and would graduate in March of 1942, as class 42-C-SE. It started out with thirteen cadets and would graduate five.

The Tuskegee Airmen

It would be April of 1943, over a year later, before the first group of pilots would be deployed. The military brass did not know what to do with them, no other squadrons wanted to fly with them because they were black and no one wanted them in their fighter groups because of segregation and the prejudices of the time. They were sent to North Africa and the Mediterranean Theater of Operations, the first group of pilots to go was the 99th Fighter Squadron

During some of their earliest missions which involved strafing and dive-bombing, the 99th Fighter Squadron was teamed with white pilots to gain combat experience. One such squadron, the 33rd Fighter Group posed serious problems for the Tuskegee Airmen. Their commander, Colonel William Momyer, tried to have the program at Tuskegee eliminated after three inexperienced pilots broke rank to chase German planes during one of their first missions. While teamed with the 33rd Squadron, the Tuskegee Airmen were segregated on base, given little or no briefing reports, and advised to "keep up." Momyer's efforts to have the Tuskegee Airmen's participation in the war reduced and his accusations would lead to a formal investigation by the McCloy Commission in 1943.

They would survive the threat presented by Momyer and soon, after their outstanding performance in Anzio, Italy, in January of 1944, would be joined by other squadrons from Tuskegee – the 100, 301st and 302nd Fighter Squadrons, collectively the 332nd Fighter

Group, and receive much fame as the "Red Tails." This group of Tuskegee pilots would consist of 450 pilots - the 99th plus the 332nd. They became famous for the protection that they provided during bomber escort missions.

Another group of pilots, the 477th Composite Fighter-Bomber Group, was also comprised of Tuskegee Airmen, but was never deployed. This group experienced a high level of discrimination and segregation; their commander was Colonel William Momyer. They were not allowed to use officers clubs even though they were officers and were constantly moved around from location to location to prevent integration. Momyer constantly schemed to avoid the occurrence of any incident that would result in a white serviceman having to take orders from a black officer. In their most famous incident, the Freeman Field "mutiny" incident, the Tuskegee Airmen pilots were classified in a manner that prevented them from using the same officers club as white pilots and essentially asked to sign an order to that affect. Many refused. When they attempted to enter an officers club designated for whites while at Freeman Field, Kentucky, 101 of them were arrested. They were charged under the "64th Article of War" for willful disobedience. During times of war, being convicted under this article could carry the death penalty. Only three men were ever tried, two were acquitted; one, Roger C. Terry was convicted and paid a $150 fine. He was issued a pardon by President Bill Clinton some fifty years later.

The 450 black pilots in the 332nd Fighter Group and the 99th Fighter Squadron who served in overseas combat earned 850 medals. They lost 66 of their members. An additional 30 were taken as prisoners of war. For every one of the Tuskegee Airmen planes that the Germans shot down, the Tuskegee Airmen shot down four of theirs. The only time a destroyer was sunk with a machine gun during the war was when it was done by two Tuskegee Airmen, Wendell Pruitt and Gwynne Pierson, of the 99th Fighter Squadron. Captain Roscoe Brown, Lieutenant Earle Lane, and Flight Officer Charles V. Brantley distinguished themselves when they became the first American pilots to shoot down German jets – one each - during the war, and they shot them down while flying propeller planes. Most important and impressive, according to the United States Army Air Corps, the Tuskegee Airmen flew more than 200 bomber escort missions and never lost a bomber that they were escorting to enemy fire. Each of the pilots was supported by ten other civilian or military men and women on the ground. The contributions of the support personnel should also be acknowledged and included as part of the Tuskegee Airman legacy.

The Tuskegee Airmen's record was so outstanding that it is widely believed that it was the main reason that President Harry Truman issued

Executive Order 9980 which established fair employment practices within the federal government and 9981 which required equal treatment and opportunities within the armed services, both in July of 1948. These orders literally integrated both the federal government and the armed services. In fact the Air Force branch of the military had begun to integrate right after it was established as a separate branch in 1947 and even before those executive orders. It their own ways, these developments paved the way for the thrust of the civil rights movement which would begin in nearby Montgomery, Alabama about eight years after the closing of Tuskegee Army Air Field.

Years after their service, perhaps Lieutenant General Benjamin O. Davis, Jr. said it best of the young men he led so proudly: "I give full marks to the Tuskegee Airmen themselves. They bore the brunt of it all. However, they could not have achieved their glorious record without lots of help. That help came from Gen. Noel Parrish, who held in his hand the key decision that blacks could fly airplanes at a superior level of proficiency; it came from "Chief" Alfred Anderson and his corps of Primary Flying School instructors, who performed their mission in exemplary fashion throughout all the years of TAAF existence; it belonged to the hundreds of officers and airmen who did the support job at Tuskegee Army Air Field, without which our combat effort could not have gone forward. I must also mention with admiration, the wives of the Tuskegee Airmen who suffered the privations of Alabama while they rendered the necessary support which their husbands needed and enjoyed through the long years of World War II."

Cadets arriving at Tuskegee were quintessentially the "talented tenth" of Dubois lore, assembled from far flung places around the nation, from the top schools, highly accomplished and among the nation's brightest young men. It was not what they got out of the program as much as what they brought to it that gives cause to speak of them.

From the Tuskegee Airmen ranks emerged an honor-roll of leaders – military standouts: General Benjamin O. Davis, Jr., the first black Air Force General, General Daniel "Chappie" James, Jr., the nation's first black four-star General, and Major General Lucius Theus who rose from the ranks of the enlisted men to be the first Black combat support officer to be promoted to brigadier general.

Their ranks also included many who went on to become civilian standouts - politicians, judges, corporate executives, educators, doctors, clergymen, entrepreneurs and members of a host of other professions. William Coleman, former secretary of transportation during the Ford administration, was a Tuskegee Airman; Coleman Young, a bombardier navigator and second lieutenant was elected the mayor of Detroit in the 1970s and 1980s, Charles Diggs, became a Congressman from Michigan, Percy Sutton, an intelligence officer, became president of the Manhattan Borough. Sutton also established the first black radio station in New York City.

One man, James O. Plinton made history in 1957 when he became the first black executive at a major airline after having been appointed executive assistant to the director of personnel at Trans World Airline. Later, Eastern Airline bought out a company that he owned and made him a vice president. He was their first black vice-president and the highest ranking black executive in the industry. About five years after Plinton was hired, Eastern hired another Tuskegee Airman by the name of Archibald Cox to supervise the mechanical engineers. Elwood Driver became Vice Chairman of the National Transportation Safety Board. Lee Archer became a vice president of General Foods.

It is important to remember that the men and women who were a part of the Tuskegee Experience and performed so outstandingly during World War II were merely trained at Tuskegee. They were not produced there. These heroes such as those who taught cadets how to become pilots, like Charles Herbert Flowers, were the product of their families, communities, institutions, and their own individual value systems. Their accomplishments are a testament to strivers and to the belief that, where humanity is concerned, the Almighty does not play favorites.

Appendix A

Citations and Other Expressions of Recognition Given to Charles Herbert Flowers, Jr.

Ebenezer United Methodist Men's Mentoring Program Recognition: Mentor of the Year, June 1991

Maryland General Assembly for Black History Month Recognition: February 21, 1997

City of Glenarden for Black History Month Proclamation: February 20, 1999

U. S. House of Representatives, August 26, 2000 Citation: August 26, 2000

Senator of Maryland Resolution: August 26, 2000

At the White House by President William J. Clinton Greetings: August 9, 2000

Tuskegee Airmen, Inc. Heritage Award: August 11, 2000

Prince Georges County Council Proclamation: August 16, 2000

U. S. House of Representatives
Salutation: August 28, 2000

NSA/CSS and Fort George G. Meade, May Recognition May 18, 2001

Glenarden Elementary School
Appreciation: February 16, 2006

Tuskegee University
 Honorary Doctorate: February 23, 2006

Tasker Middle School
Appreciation: February 27, 2006

Virginia Military Institute
Recognition: July 21, 2006

United States. Congress
Congressional Gold Medal of Honor: March 29, 2007

E. J. Williams Lodge 14
32nd Degree in Masonry: March 31, 2007

Sojourner-Douglass College
Gold Medal Award: June 1, 2007

Omega Psi Phi Fraternity, Inc., North Carolina
Recognition: October 14, 2007

Student Government - Charles H. Flowers High School
Recognition: "Charles Herbert Flowers Day," November 14, 2007

Maryland 4th District Congressman Alvin Wynn
Proclamation: "November 14, 2007 is Charles Herbert Flowers Day",

Maryland State Senator Nathaniel Exum and Maryland State Delegate
Michael Vaughn, 24th Legislative District of Prince Georges's County
Proclamations: Congratulations on "Charles Herbert Flowers Day,"
November 14, 2007

Ebenezer United Methodist Church
Recipient of the "Man of the Year" for Men's Day at Ebenezer United
Methodist Church, November 9, 2008.

Maryland General Assembly
Official Citation of Recognition for Aviation History Month
November 25, 2008

Student Government Association, Charles Flowers High School
Lifetime Accomplishment Award
November 25, 2008

Appendix B
Charles Herbert Flowers, Jr.'s Family Tree

Maternal:

Great Grandparents: Enos Huntley and Wife (Name Unknown)
             Children: John, Sallie, Roxana, and Jamie

Grandparents: John and Lula Brewer Huntley
             Children: Ola and Charles Flowers –
                          1 son , Charles H. Flowers, Jr.
                  Robert and Leona Bynum – 1 son
                  Anabell and Charles Smith – 2 daughters
                  Beulah Huntley – No children
                  Allean and James Steele – 1 daughter
                  Lester and Ella Huntley – No children
                  Thomas and Elizabeth Huntley – No children
                  Jeretha and Julius Little – No children
                  Leroy and Rose Huntley – 1 son
                  Joseph and Penny Huntley – 1 son

Note: All of Herb's cousins on his mother's side of the family grew up and attended schools in New York City except Robert's son who grew up in Providence, R. I. Herb did spend a lot of time with his mother's youngest brother, Joseph, who did not move to New York until after finishing high school in 1931.

Paternal:

Great Grandparents: Unknown

Grand Parents – William and Mary Flowers
  Children: Gillie and Alex Douglas – 7 children
     Tommie Flowers – No children
     Eliza and Jerry Teal – 10 children
     Walter and Effie Flowers – 10 children
     Wencie and Arthur Liles – 10 children
     Ida and Sandy Marshall – 10 children
     William Flowers, Jr. – No children
     Lester and Gussie Flowers – 9 children
     George and Lina Flowers – 2 children
     Charles and Ola Huntley Flowers – 1 child
        Charles Herbert Flowers, Jr.
     Delphia and Joe Bennett – 10 children

Note: The cousins who attended high school with Herb were Rena Flowers, Clarence Flowers, Marie Flowers, Joleitha Bennett, and Charles Bennett.

References

Air Force Link Biographies, Brigadier General Frederick V. H. Kimble, Retrieved September 12, 2007 from http://www.af.mil/bios

Casablanca Multimedia, Tuskegee Airmen History, Retrieved April 9, 2007 from http://www.tuskegee.airmen.org

Negro Airmen International, Inc., About Us, Retrieved September 3, 2007 from http://www.blackwings.com/about.html

Negro Airmen International, Inc., History, Retrieved April 9, 2007 from http://www.blackwings.com/history.html

ParkNet, National Park Service, The Tuskegee Airmen—Overview: Legends of Tuskegee, Retrieved March 16, 2007 from http://www.cr.nps.gov/museum/exhibits/Tuskegee/airoverview.htm

Smith, Clarence D., History of the East Coast Chapter, Tuskegee Airmen, Inc., Retrieved April 9, 2007 from http://www.ecctai.com/ecc/ecchistory.htm

Chapter 11: Written by George Norfleet, Robnor Publishing; five photos courtesy of Robnor Publishing.